ACORNPRESS

Epekwitk Mi'kmaq Poetry

From Prince Edward Island

L'nu Poems and Art

by Julie Pellissier-Lush

2021

Epekwitk Mi'kmaq Poetry from Prince Edward Island
Copyright © Julie Pellissier-Lush, 2021
ISBN 978-1-77366-085-1

Cover design by Kenny Vail
Interior design by Cassandra Aragonez
Editing by Dianne Hicks Morrow
Printed in Canada by Marquis

Library and Archives Canada Cataloguing in Publication

Title: Epekwitk : Mi'kmaq poetry from Prince Edward Island
/ L'nu poems and art by Julie Pellissier-Lush.

Names: Pellissier-Lush, Julie, 1970- author, artist.
Identifiers: Canadiana (print) 20210317019 | Canadiana (ebook) 20210317043 |
ISBN 9781773660851 (softcover) | ISBN 9781773660868 (HTML)

Subjects: LCGFT: Poetry.

Classification: LCC PS8631.E4684 E64 2021 | DDC C811/.6—dc23

The publisher acknowledges the support of the Government of Canada,
the Canada Council for the Arts and the Province of Prince Edward Island for
our publishing program.

Canada Council   Conseil des Arts
for the Arts   du Canada

P.O. Box 22024
Charlottetown, Prince Edward Island
C1A 9J2

Acornpress.ca

ACORNPRESS

Dedication:

This book is dedicated to all poets, writers and storytellers who need faith to learn that your words matter, because they do! Today is the day for all of you to start writing, to start sharing your stories. Everyone has a story just waiting to be told, something that keeps dancing around their heart until it is ready to explode onto a paper or computer screen. Keep doing what you are doing, believe in yourself because amazing things are just waiting around the corner for every one of you, just believe in yourself and start writing!

This is also dedicated to my family, your love and faith always helps me to write more, and to share more stories.

TABLE OF CONTENTS

PART 1 - TEACHINGS

PART 2 - GHOST STORIES

PART 3 - PRAYERS

PART 4 -MY FAMILY

PART 5 - TAKING A STAND

The Poetry

For many years Julie has written poetry, some poems were created with teachings from our Elder. Some were created to learn more about this wonderful art: Learning how to take words from my heart and bring them to my head and move them out onto paper so my words can touch the heart of another. The gift of poetry is we can take what you like, use what we need, and most of all enjoy it!

Thank you to Novalea for helping with the first draft and giving me strength to move forward with this work, and Dianne for making everything as perfect as it could be your dedication and love could be felt behind every email.

The Art

About three years ago my cousin, Pam, showed me how to make drop art, you take your favorite colours and white glue, and you drop it onto your canvas and skillfully move the exploding bubbles of colour into patterns that make you happy. These are some that I have done while first learning and some that were made just for this book. The best part of this art is that through your own eyes you will see what you need to explain why they were selected for each poem. I do hope you like them- they make me very happy!

A great big thank you to Savanna Rayner-Lewis for the beautiful Purple Ribbon art and to my Goddaughter Makayla Bernard, who made the beautiful quillwork art. Thank you for being a part of my very first poetry book! Wela'lin!!

TEACHINGS

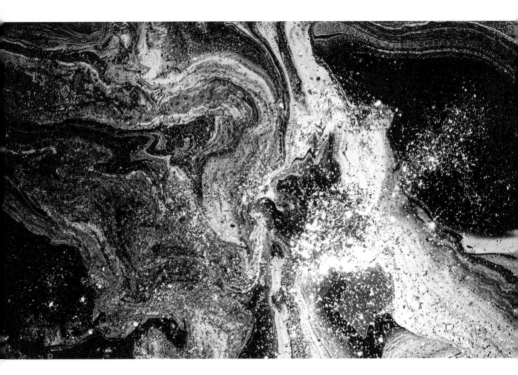

CULTURE AND TRADITION

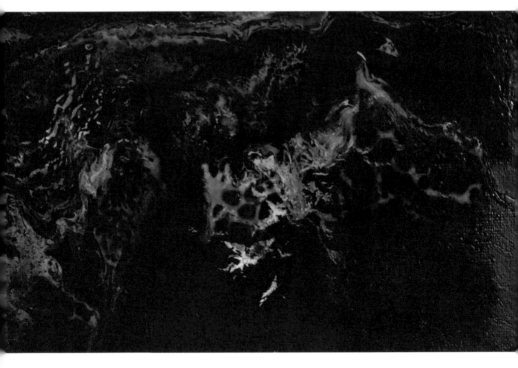

LITTLE GRASS DANCER

Culture and Tradition

Culture and tradition – what are they to me?
A way to help your heart to see
Culture is the root of who you are
Who you pray to, who your family is—near or far
How you regenerate your heart and your mind
How you prepare for a really, really hard time
It is not how you dress, or you do up your hair
It is what you feel in your heart when you share
Tradition is how things have always been done
From our ceremonies to how we all welcome the sun
From our spirituality to our prayers – to our dance, craft, and song
The traditions we have will help keep us strong
As individuals, as family, as community, and as a nation
Our culture and traditions need to be passed on to our next generations
If we share it, and save it in our hearts and our minds
It will live longer than our children and grandchildren this time

Little Grass Dancer

My little grass dancer dances so tall
My little grass dancer dances although he is small
He dances around without saying a word
He raises his arms up just like a bird
Stomping his feet to bless the sacred ground
My little grass dancer moves around and around
My little grass dancer crouches and spreads his arms out
Now he looks at the elders to see what they are all about
The beautiful colours of blue-white and red
An image of the eagle appears in his head
He picked out the colours, the eagle feather for his chest
His legs are all ready now, no time for him to rest
To show his love of the creator, his community, his nation
He will continue to dance for his generation

What makes you brave?

What makes you brave is what's inside
To talk of those things, you'd rather hide
To be a young man and wear your hair in a braid
To keep your head up when you are afraid
To work hard in school to get a good grade
To stand up for things when you'd rather sit down
To be yourself even when friends are around
To know and share your stories from the past
To realize that worst times don't last
To be brave can be hard and keep you up through the night
But just know what you are doing is not wrong, it is right!

I am just in need of help; my throat feels sore and raw
I keep my head looking to the ground

The Jingle Dress

Jingle jungle jangle
As her dress moves up and down

Jingle jungle jangle
As her feet softly touch the ground

Jingle jungle jangle
Are the sounds her dress does sing

Jingle jungle jangle
Is the gift her dance does bring

Around and around the dancer, moves her body to the beat
Everyone can hear the pretty sounds created by her feet
Her dress was made by loving hands and shows a story of our past

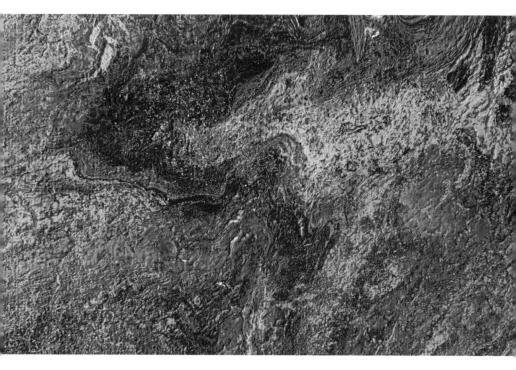

WHAT MAKES YOU BRAVE?

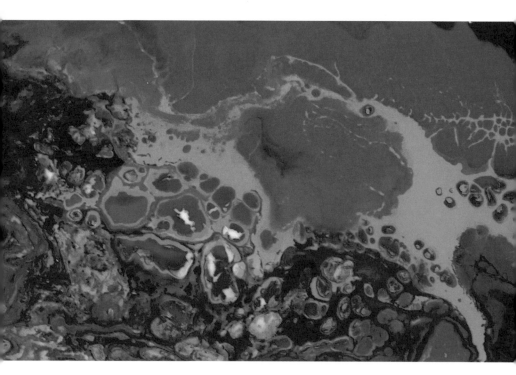

THE JINGLE DREAM

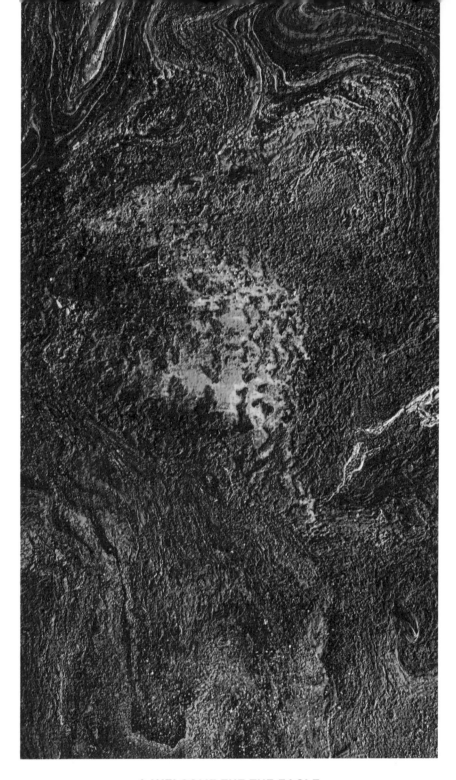

A WELCOME THE THE EAGLE

A Welcome to the Eagle

Beautiful eagle flying so high
Blessing this gathering as you glide by
Let me explain a Mawiomi from start to end
The "Grand Entry" is how the whole day begins
With flags carried by elders with so much heart and pride
All the people are here now and the ancestors too

Beautiful eagle flying so high
Blessing this gathering as you glide by

The drummers are drumming
So loud and so strong
Singing in Mi'kmaq the whole weekend long
The host drum will lead the way
All will take turns throughout the day

Beautiful eagle flying so high
Blessing this gathering as you glide by

The dancers are dancing around and around
All with beautiful regalia, some so long they touch the ground
Some with jingles that make music all on their own
Different types of regalia worn by the dancers, from small to full grown

Beautiful eagle flying so high
Blessing this gathering as you glide by

Crafters and vendors all wait for guests to stop by
They hope you will give some of their crafts a try
With food, jewelry, and baskets you can find
You can see what you need there, all "one of a kind"

Beautiful eagle flying so high
Blessing this gathering as you glide by

The volunteers sweat while preparing the food
No one will go hungry— the smells make everyone drool
Their hard work can be tasted each night
They all work together to make food that delights

Beautiful eagle flying so high
Blessing this gathering as you glide by

The Master of Ceremonies rallies the crowd
The dancers and drummers listen as he stands proud
He tells them when to stop and when to begin
He will make the crowd laugh or at least grin

Beautiful eagle flying so high
Blessing this gathering as you glide by

The elders sit in comfort, they sit in the shade
They watch, they listen and sometimes they smile
If you talk to them without being afraid, you will learn
They know it is time for this beautiful culture to return

Beautiful eagle flying so high
Blessing this gathering as you glide by

The children all gather
They run and they play
They have so much fun
They smile all day

Beautiful eagle flying so high
Blessing this gathering as you glide by

The drummers the dancers the elders and all
Give thanks to the Eagle as they stand so tall
To the eagle who only comes once in a while
Thank you for coming and making us smile

Beautiful eagle please tell the Creator today

Thank you for helping us celebrate this way

A Way to Find the Pride Inside

When I go to see a doctor
I keep my head looking to the ground
As I sit in the waiting room
I keep my head looking to the ground
They call my name to register me in
I glimpse disapproval in their eyes
I keep my head looking to the ground
I mumble my name and wait for them to let me sit
I keep my head looking to the ground

When I go in the nurse looks around the room like she is doing an inventory
I keep my head looking to the ground
Why do I feel so judged by these people on how I look or dress?
I keep my head looking to the ground
With all the eyes that see right through me why can't I just disappear?
I keep my head looking to the ground
Am I alone in thinking that I am a good person too?
I keep my head looking to the ground
I am just in need of help; my throat feels sore and raw
I keep my head looking to the ground
I do not drink or do drugs but money I have not
I keep my head looking to the ground
Please give me strength to someday stand tall, I pray
I keep my head looking to the ground
I am more than just these faded jeans and second-hand shirt
I keep my head looking to the ground

A knock on the door startles my thoughts
I keep my head looking to the ground
His eyes of brown with a long dark braid hung over his white coat
I could not keep my head looking to the ground
He smiles and really looks at me and asks me how I am
I keep my head looking at this doctor who is talking to me
I point to my throat, but I can't say a word
I keep my head looking at this doctor who is looking at me

You will be alright young man, he says, and for once I truly believe it
I can be anything I want - just wait my friends and you will see it

I leave the doctor's that day with my head lifted high
I let my braid fall down my back from its home inside my hat
I keep my head looking straight ahead
I smile at people who walk by and they smile back at me
I keep my head looking straight ahead
I found a pride, a way to dream so I am all right now inside
I keep my head looking straight ahead to the future I now can see
I am a First Nations man and there is a world of possibilities for me
I do not drink or do drugs but money I have not
I keep my head looking to the ground
Please give me strength to someday stand tall, I pray
I keep my head looking to the ground
I am more than just these faded jeans and second-hand shirt
I keep my head looking to the ground

A knock on the door startles my thoughts
I keep my head looking to the ground
His eyes of brown with a long dark braid hung over his white coat
I could not keep my head looking to the ground
He smiles and really looks at me and asks me how I am
I keep my head looking at this doctor who is talking to me
I point to my throat, but I can't say a word
I keep my head looking at this doctor who is looking at me
You will be alright young man, he says, and for once I truly believe it
I can be anything I want - just wait my friends and you will see it

I leave the doctor's that day with my head lifted high
I let my braid fall down my back from its home inside my hat
I keep my head looking straight ahead
I smile at people who walk by and they smile back at me
I keep my head looking straight ahead
I found a pride, a way to dream so I am all right now inside
I keep my head looking straight ahead to the future I now can see

I am a First Nations man and there is a world of possibilities for me

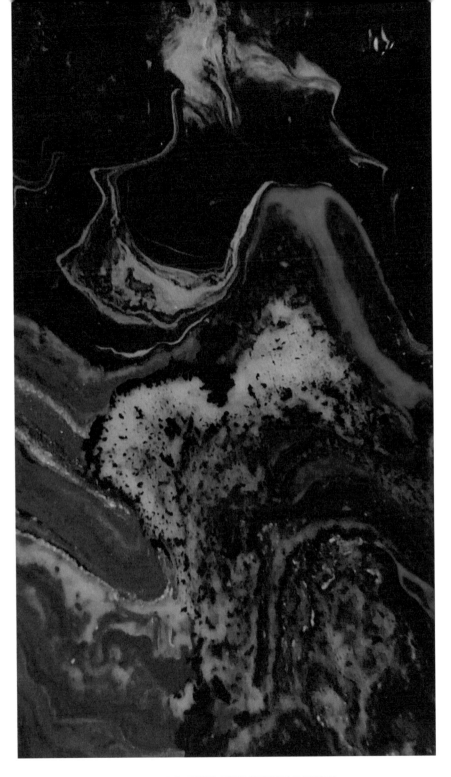

A WAY TO FIND THE PRIDE INSIDE

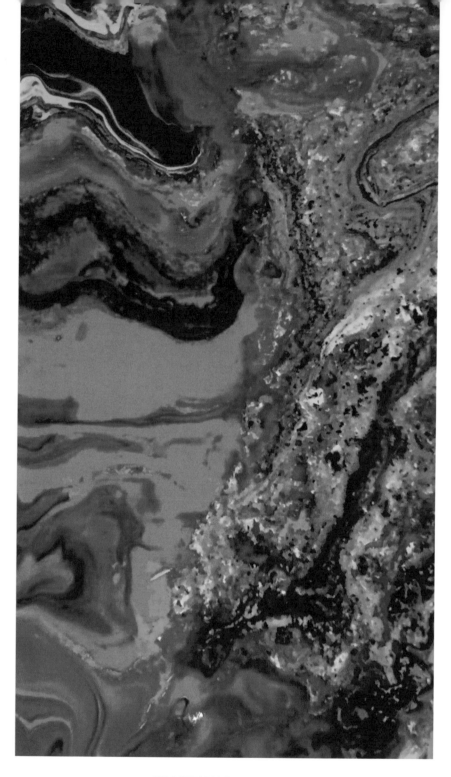

GRANDMOTHER MOON

Grandmother Moon

Grandmother Moon in the dark night sky
I see your light from way up high
You connect us to our ancestors when the sun goes down
When it is dark, they do not stay around

They leave the moon to look after us at night
To enhance their intuition and send messages while we sleep tight
Grandmother Moon's connection with the water and the tide
Is not the only thing she must look after outside

The creatures of the night listen for her wisdom and guidance
She does this even though all we hear is Calm... White... Silence...
I stare up at you each night to see you grow bigger until you are full
Your cycle affects us women with the power that you pull

What do you look like behind that beautiful white moonlight?
Are you a wise old woman with long gray hair?
Or a beautiful young woman with a face that is fair?
You are a mystery, but I do pray that you come to me this night

Look down at me from way up high and show me what I do is right.
Visit me in my sleep and send me your wisdom as I dream tonight
This is all I can really say because the teachings are not mine
Dear reader, if you want to know more, go to an Elder
and spend some time

Many things I have learned cannot go in print when it
comes to our culture
It must be something we share verbally with one other
Grandmother Moon, our guardian, our voice of reason
You look after all your children of the red earth no matter the season

As your journey across the sky comes to an end this night
I will think of you with love and wait for the next twilight
Goodnight Grandmother Moon,
I will see you in my dreams when I close my eyes
May you have a peaceful journey as you cross the night sky.

Our Four Colours

Red

Red is the colour of our Island, so beautiful surrounded by the waves
Red is the colour of our sunsets as the day turns into night
Red is the colour of our life's blood, keeping us healthy and strong
Red is the colour of our hearts where our souls and our love are centered
Red is the colour of our anger, venting, raging and wild
Red is the colour of our people, so beautiful noble and proud

Yellow

Yellow is the colour of the sun, warm bright and clean
Yellow is the youth who struggle to find their path
Yellow is the spring- new life, new plants in creation
Yellow is the colour of my creativity when I look for the right word
Yellow is the colour of the fields when the dandelions come full bloom
Yellow is the colour of joy, excitement for everything new and beautiful

Black

Black is the colour of the night when we all need to get our rest
Black is the colour of our warriors, our leaders, crafters, and artists
Black is the colour of my energy because it is the colour that has all colours
Black is the colour of the west with the warm winds,
and beautiful sunsets
Black is the colour of my mind as it rests my present
and connects me to my ancestors

White

White is the colour of the snow, quiet and deep
White is the colour of our elders' hair, wise and strong
White is the colour of the north, lonely, quiet, and free
White is the colour of our knowledge, our traditions, and stories we keep
White is the language I speak as my Mi'kmaq words are lost

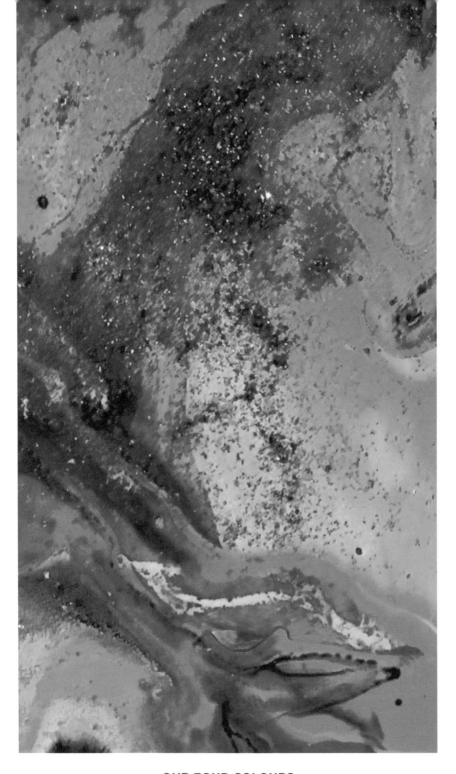

OUR FOUR COLOURS

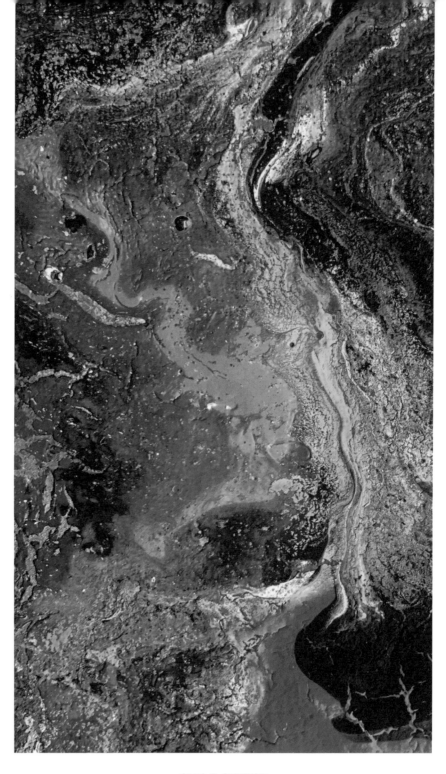

CHILD SWEEP

Child Sweep

My baby, my baby
Where are you tonight?
After I was born, I left the hospital, really late, by car
I am not sure where I was going, but not very far

My baby, my baby
Where are you tonight?
I can now say "Mommy" and I am learning how to walk
I think my parents love me because they smile when I talk

My baby, my baby
Where are you tonight?
Today I am turning two, I am still tiny and small
Sometimes I get so angry, but my parents catch me when I fall

My baby, my baby
Where are you tonight?
Today I am turning three and preschool is a horror
Today I was bad, and I had to go to sit in the corner

My baby, my baby
Where are you tonight?

I am six today and I feel like a fool
I was called a wagon burner today in school

My baby, my baby
Where are you tonight?
I am ten today, and I do not really feel the same
The kids will not let me play in their fun and games

My baby, my baby
Where are you tonight?
I am twelve today, Mom and I heard my parents say
It is not our fault, she is not ours, let us send her on her way

My baby, my baby
Where are you tonight?

I am thirteen now, and I have a friend who is nineteen
He says he loves me, and he is everything I have dreamed

My baby, my baby
Where are you tonight?
Today I am fourteen Mama, and I am going to have a baby
I am not sure why everyone keeps calling me crazy?

My baby, my baby
Where are you tonight?
I am fifteen today and they took away my baby
I am taking drugs sometimes to make my days go hazy

My baby, my baby
Where are you tonight?
I am sixteen today and need money all the time
Police know me, but why is being native part of my crime?

My baby, my baby
Where are you tonight?
I thought of looking for you today
Not sure why you gave me away

My baby, my baby
Where are you tonight?
Mommy oh mommy, I am nineteen right now
Trying to get better, I just need help to learn how

My baby, my baby
Where are you tonight?
On a plane coming to you in PEI tonight
To find my roots and try and make everything alright

My baby, my baby
I cannot believe I am holding you tonight
Here I am Mom, and I think that now I will be alright
Now sit with me please, and just hold me tight.

The Drummer

The Honour Song is floating in the air around me
The group drums together, singing so free
Their history through drumming and song
The words they echo so loud, and so strong

One young man stands out, so I look over to see him
Eyes closed, head tilted up, his mouth has a grin
Hitting the drum with a regular beat
His Mom looks at him, so proud in her seat

The drumming and song float up to the sky
I look to the heavens and wonder why—
Why is this music so special each time?
Why does it fill our hearts and our minds?

After the drumming was done for a while
That drummer came over and sat with a smile
If you want, I can tell you what makes this song great
Why when you hear it you want to celebrate

When we are children, adults, and teens
We hear the drum and somehow it cleans
Our hearts, our minds and our souls
No matter if we are young or old

The sound of the drum goes deep inside of me
Thank you, drummer, for helping me see
What the drum really means and why
First time I heard it, it made me cry

It is the sound of our people, our mothers, and fathers
It is the sound of our people, our sisters, and brothers—
I can hear it in the Mi'kmaq words you sing under the sun
I can hear it in the pulsating beat of the drum

To ground us in our history, and give us wings to soar
Into the future, as a Nation who could ask for more
Please drum some more for all of us gathered today
Come back into the circle once more and play

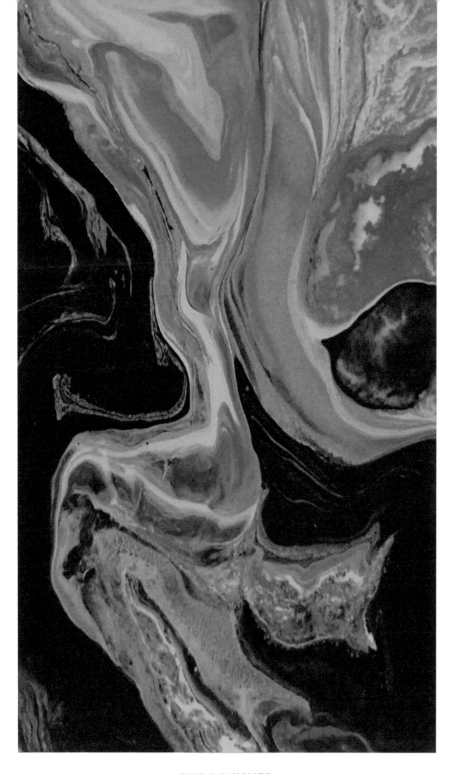

THE DRUMMER

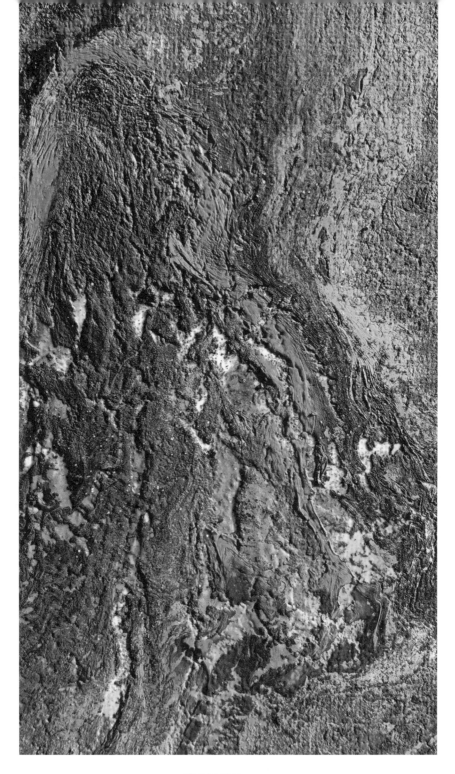

THE FEATHER

The Feather

I was given a beautiful feather just the other day
From an Eagle that was white, brown, and gray

An elder presented it to me
With smiling eyes, he said it was meant to be

He blessed the feather in a smudge and said
A feather is much like our life, as he tapped it on my head

The feather's centre rib shows the path we all must take
The other little ribs are the choices we must make

If you do not stay on the right path as you should
Things get complicated and it is harder to stay good

This is a gift you must treasure. Hold these teachings in your heart forever
A lady from Summerside made me a beautiful red case for my feather

Do not drop this precious gift from the creator
Or you will have to give it away later

For if this gift should ever fall
It wasn't really yours at all

These are just some of those things I know
Of how a feather can help me grow

Maybe someday I will be given another
This special gift is truly like no other

The Braid - a poetic explanation!

When I see a man with a braid on one of my adventures
Be it a lawyer, a crafter, a drummer, or a dancer
I wonder who they wear this symbol for so
I start asking some questions and then I ask some more

The answers help me figure out
What Mi'kmaq braids are all about
When it is time to sit and do their braid
They take three parts all neatly laid

With the first part, they say a prayer for their heart
May it be strong and loving right from the start
May the warmth of love spread over me today
And come out in what I do and say

The second part, they say a prayer for their mind
'Please help me think of good things most of the time'
The third part they say a prayer for their soul
For their spirit within to keep them whole

With each part of the hair filled with hope for the day
They are pulled all together and intertwined that way
To connect the heart, mind, and soul
To keep the man strong is what I've been told

Where is the Creator in all this ritual I say?
He is in the braid when it is all together for the day
Sweet grass is braided the same way, of course
All tied together with no remorse

This medicine has prayers inside
To be used by the Mi'kmaq with pride
So, when you see a braid worn outside
Or a braid of sweet grass beautifully tied

Just know there is a lot of preparation
Involved in this aboriginal celebration
Heart, mind, and soul together
Just like the blessing of a sacred feather

This is our tradition and who we are inside
When our men wear their braids with such pride

THE BRAID

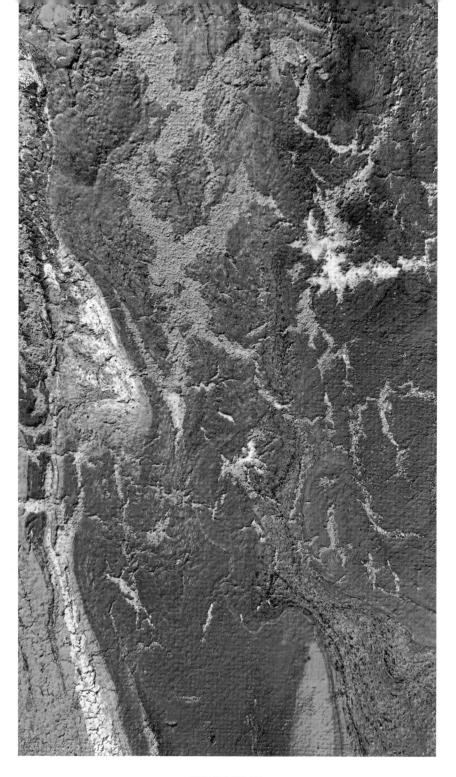

WABANAKI

Wabanaki — The People from where the Sun Rises

Since the beginning of time, the Creator looked after the Wabanaki;
the People from the East.
With love and guidance, all that they needed
was forever within their reach
The animals, the plants and the medicines were all there in three-fold
No one went without because they listened to what they'd been told

The People knew these were gifts from the Creator.
They respected the earth and her plenty
Every night the Wabanaki People gave thanks for
having no belly left empty
The ancestors shared all their knowledge and skill with each generation
The wisdom they learned since the dawn of creation

Their stories and songs were always quiet teachings
Their eyes saw the future with so many weeping
They are all with us now. We can call on them when in despair
Sometimes, if we are lucky, we can glimpse their gray hair

Today the Wabanaki people are searching for the past
Looking for their history in every blade of grass

The history of our people is like the sand on the beach
with each grain having a story to teach
We look to our past so our tomorrows will be bright
and tomorrows are always within our sight

To create a future for our youth and all the babies to come
To be as warm and as bright as the beautiful sun
With our help now they will be stronger and wiser with each generation
The People of the East stand proud with the youth we see in our Nation
Our youth know the culture and they share our traditions with pride
For many years that was missing—now it is alive
In the hearts and minds of our young, that knowledge survives.

The Wabanaki people are the first to see the day
Our bodies and hearts molded from the red clay
The future is now in what we do and we say
Please bless all our people, Creator, I pray

The Rain

Small drops are falling from the sky today
As a child, rain would always make me sad
Thinking of things, I now couldn't play
Frustrated me and made me mad

Small drops are falling from the sky today
As a teen, they didn't bother me too much
I had books to read, and my friends could still gather
To me, getting drenched really didn't matter

Small drops are falling from the sky today
As an adult, seeing the rain gave me a fright—
Watching pets and kids race into my clean house
Dripping wet, muddy, and full of delight

Small drops are falling from the sky today
Now that I am older, I can truly see
How wonderful the rain can really be—
It feeds our plants and our flowers
Fills our wells, our oceans, and it cleans
The air and the land, gathering all the dust.
Rain keeps us all healthy and our trees all green

Small drops are falling from the sky today
Scientists say our tears are different when we cry
From happiness, a broken heart, fear, or love.
Elders say when you cry the tears must trickle down
Like the rain from the sky
This will help to take away our pain
I do not know why— that is a teaching for another day
I just know I must listen to what our elders say

Small drops are falling from the sky today
I think I should go outside and play
Let the rain clean my body my heart and my soul
I honour those small drops that fall from the sky today

THE RAIN

OUR ELDERS

Our Elders

Elders, oh elders, where are you now?
Do you sit and wait for us to come to you in need?
Where do you keep all your knowledge, your stories, your wisdom?
Elders oh, elders where are you now?

Who are the elders whose hearts hold the past
with the stories from time untold?
With gray hair and soft voices, they council
and lead with the wisdom they hold.
They can see our people now,
from the past and in the future.
Traditionally they taught the youth,
counselled the leaders and looked out for all.
Now they sit with history in their hearts –
waiting for someone to learn what they know.

Elders, oh elders, where are you now?
Do you sit and wait for us to come to you in need?
Where do you keep all your knowledge, your stories, your wisdom?
Elders, oh elders where are you now?

Their eyes, full of wisdom, some lost and alone
To be an elder, I've heard that you don't have to be old.
I look to you now to hear the stories and the knowledge you hold,
So, I can learn it and share it, because it needs to be told.

My children, my children, where are you now?
Is there a place in your heart missing?
It is the voice of your elder you need.
They will give you wisdom, love, and guidance
and maybe plant a seed.

Oh children, oh children, where are you now?
To learn your history and know your stories
We need to listen, even if it is only an hour

Elders, oh elders, where are you now?

Do you want to know?

Elders, oh elders, where are you now?
Do you want to understand?

This is why I do what I do
Or talk the way I talk

Do you want to know?
Do you want to understand?

Sometimes when I don't respond
It is not because I have nothing to say

Do you want to know?
Do you want to understand?

When I am angry, I may not tell you why
But when I am ready I will—then I will probably cry

Do you want to know?
Do you want to understand?

I have been told by the elders that our words are so strong
Angry words can knock even a healthy person down

Do you want to know?
Do you want to understand?

Protect yourself with positive feelings and thoughts
Stay close to people who keep you safe and loved

Do you want to know?
Do you want to understand?

Our work is our family for eight hours a day
We may not get along, but we can show respect

Do you want to know?
Do you want to understand?

We cannot tear each other down, instead work for the same goals
We need unity to move forward in the right way

Thank you for wanting to know
I hope I can help you understand

DO YOU WANT TO KNOW?

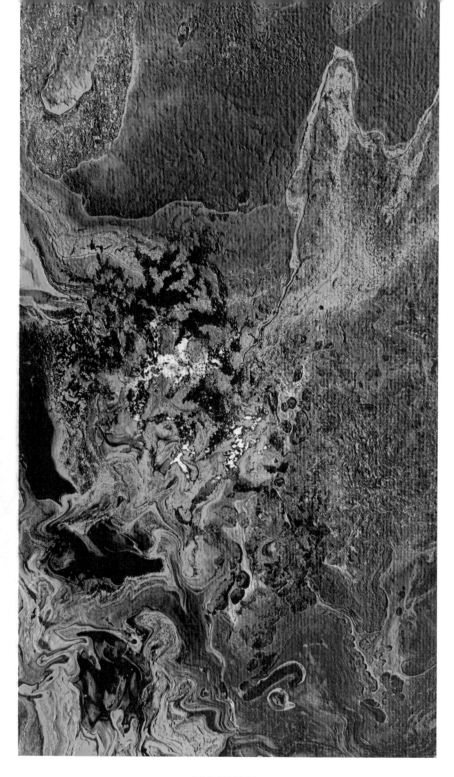

THE WIND

The Wind

I feel the wind flow into my soul

It brings the salty sea air around me and through me
Like the smoke from my smudge bowl when I pray

I feel the wind

It blows my hair this way and that—I thank the Creator above
For the wind clears my mind, fills my heart with hope and love.

I feel the wind

I close my eyes and I see my yesterdays and smile at all I have survived
I see in my mind what brought me all my joy, what makes me glad I'm alive

I feel the wind

The birth of my children, their graduations, the love I give and the love I get
I think of all my special days and hours, and I smile without regret

I feel the wind

I look to my feet, and I see my sorrows, the loss of the people that cared
People who always loved me, and those memories that we shared

I feel the wind

Hurt by leaving special places behind, every house and every lane
Each loss will always fill my eyes and cause my heart real pain

I feel the wind

I look straight ahead to my future. I cannot hide
I see things that make me worry but I face those challenges with pride

I feel the wind
The Creator only gives us what we can handle—all I can do is sigh
I am not afraid. I am going to walk to the future with my head held high

I feel the wind flow into my soul

It brings the salty sea air around me and through me
Like the smoke from my smudge bowl when I pray

I feel the wind

The Wise Chief

In the small community there were once two warriors so brave
They did not get along and soon started calling each other names
Then they began to fight one day after another
The two young men were so angry they tried to kill each other
The community could feel their hate grow bigger and bigger
Everyone supported their friends, each one picking a side
Soon the hole in the community became a huge divide
The Chief of these people was old and quite wise
He knew there must be a plan that he had to devise
For three days and four hours he crafted a wise plan
A beautiful bow and arrow he made with only his hands
So unique you could only use them when together
He would give one to each brave warrior to show
they could work together
The next morning, he called in the two warriors
Giving one the bow, the other the arrow, he smiled and said
Go out and do not come back 'til you learn how to hunt with these
No other weapons can you take for the hunt, but this one I made
Go now and find a way to be brothers
You will soon learn that you need each other to bring us back food.

The two warriors took their gifts—
with heads down they left the camp together
Bringing no other weapons than what they had in their hands
The first day they walked without even stopping
They took turns growling at each other instead of talking
For the next few days, they hunted without any luck
With their skills they could not even shoot a duck
After a week of no food, not trying to work together
They got hungry, then angry, and then even mad
One took a branch and tried to build his own bow
The other found twigs to make arrows, you know
They tried and they tried, but the parts would not fit
So, all they could do was look at the wood sadly and sit.

Look here, my angry brother, we need to make a plan,
One tired warrior finally said to the other hungry man,
I will take your bow and hunt us a deer so we can go.
The other warrior looked at him and with a snarl said NO!
Why do you get to hunt and I, not hunt a bit?
I think that I would rather we just stay here and sit.

Another day the sun rose and crossed the sky
Soon both warriors were starting to question why
They were fighting over who would go out to hunt
It really was hard work to find any animals to kill
And if they did not eat soon, they would both get very ill
Alright, take my bow and go get us some food, said one.
They both smiled as they shared this moment or two—
They thought they knew now what they had to do.
The warrior took the bow and then lifted the arrow
But alone he could not make it shoot, not even at a sparrow
One had to hold the bow in the position to shoot
The other had to hold the arrow just ready to fly
After some hours of practice, they were ready to hunt

The creator took pity on the warriors right then
A huge doe soon walked gingerly into their glen
With four arms at the ready that arrow did fly
It landed straight into the doe right before their eyes.
That night the hunters ate just like the Chiefs of old
Each mouthful of food was way better than gold
They slept side by side with their bow and their arrow
They did not wake till the sun was high overhead
They prepared the rest of their feast to bring to their Chief
Who smiled at the lesson the young warriors had learned
He never asked for his gifts to be returned
The lesson was the people had to work together
Be strong brothers until the end of forever
Their love of each other is now what they treasure
That arrow and that bow were passed down to their sons
With the lesson that the whole community is one.

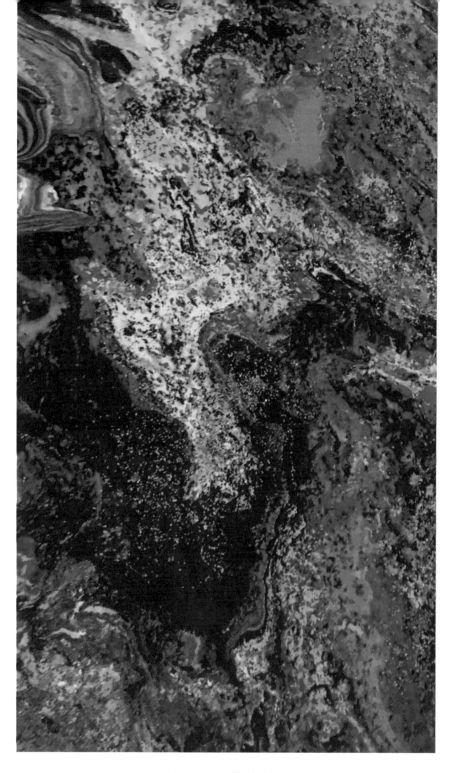

THE WISE CHEF

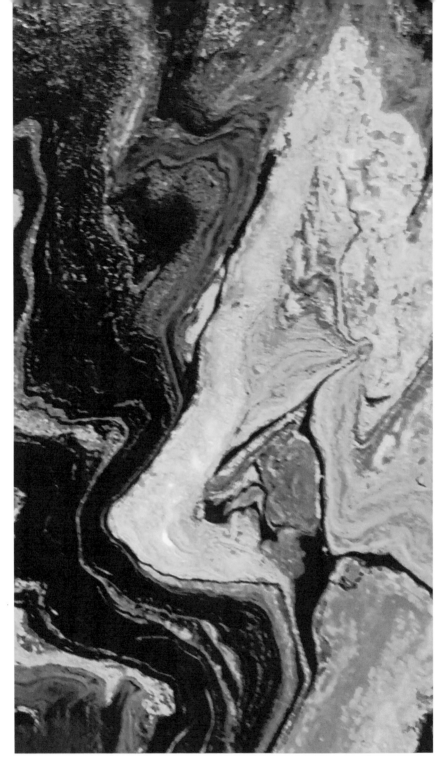

THE SOUNDS OF MAKING A BASKET

The Sounds of Making a Basket

Pounding, groaning, pounding
As ash separates, ring by ring

Scrape, scratch, scrape
As knife scrapes the strips clean

Splash, bubble, splash
As the strips soak to soften

Scratch, whoosh, scratch
As strips weave in and out

Swish, swoosh, swish
As the sweetgrass gets tied in

Groan, sigh, groan
As tired fingers pull down dried rows

Bliss, joy, bliss—
The finished basket is held up with pride

A Mother You Are

No matter what happened
The past is the past
Be strong and remember
You are loved and so needed
A mother you are

Forgive yourself and be firm and strong
Move forward and know
They will love you forever and still need you so much
A strong Mi'kmaq Mother with a big heart
A mother you are

With the story of your family that needs to be told
Share with your children what is in your heart
Live each day like it is a gift from the Creator
Each moment a treasure that you can remember forever
Give your child all your love because now you are together
A mother you are, my friend
And always will be

A MOTHER YOU ARE

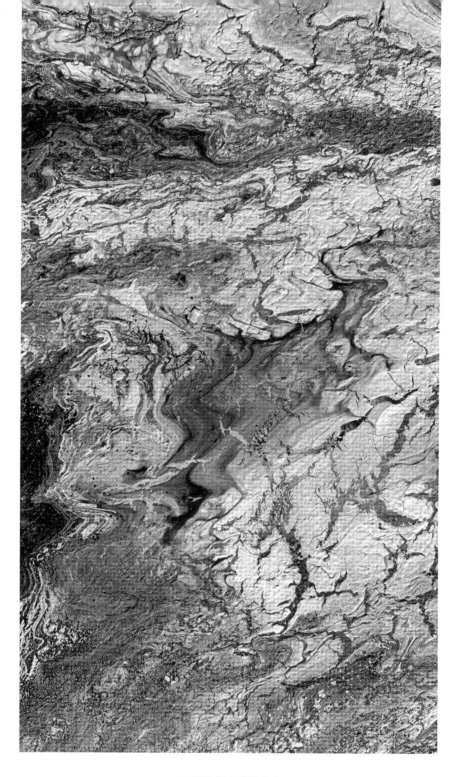

THE SANDHILLS

The Sandhills

The Sandhills take me back to being a little girl—
Long white beaches and sunsets that make your toes curl
Blueberries and cranberries enough to fill your tum
But enough mosquitos to make you want to run

White beautiful dunes of sand
History under the land
Hundreds-of-years-old campsites set up at last light
Where Mi'kmaq people always stopped to stay the night
They would rest, and hunt and fish
Walrus, seal, and lobster—more than one could wish

It has been a summer place for so long
Where the Mi'kmaq people stayed and got strong
Would the women sit there and make clothes on the shore?
Would the men mend their nets and carve arrowheads and more?
When the sun goes down and the campfires lit
It is here on this Island with the ancestors I sit

If you listen at night while you sit on the beach
Mi'kmaq words float around you but just out of reach
If you are awake on a quiet evening out there
You can hear footsteps and soft breathing in the air
The ancestors come to see what their people are up to today
So always be respectful of what you might say

On the beaches of the Sandhills, my childhood playground home
When I was there my ancestors were always around
Close your eyes right now if you dare
Can you smell the beautiful salty sea air?
The wind blowing your hair all around
Seashells you can pick up all over the ground

The Sandhills is where you can still find volcanic rock
The place my imagination begins with stories of a fox
For a ceremony to cleanse your mind heart and soul
You must offer a smudge from a very special bowl
A place where maybe young warriors were given a quest
Or maybe an eagle or two built their nests
And this is also where my beach poem will rest.

Maybe Someday

While I sit at work, I think to myself, maybe someday

While I drive home, I think to myself, maybe someday

While I cook dinner at night, I think to myself, maybe someday

While I brush my teeth at night, I think to myself, maybe someday

While I climb into bed, I think to myself, maybe someday

As I lie down and slowly fall asleep, I live all my maybe some days

One after another...
I am a doctor, a lawyer, a lover, a fighter, an actress
A poet, and in my dreams, this is where my "some days" come true...

While I wake up the morning, I think to myself, maybe someday

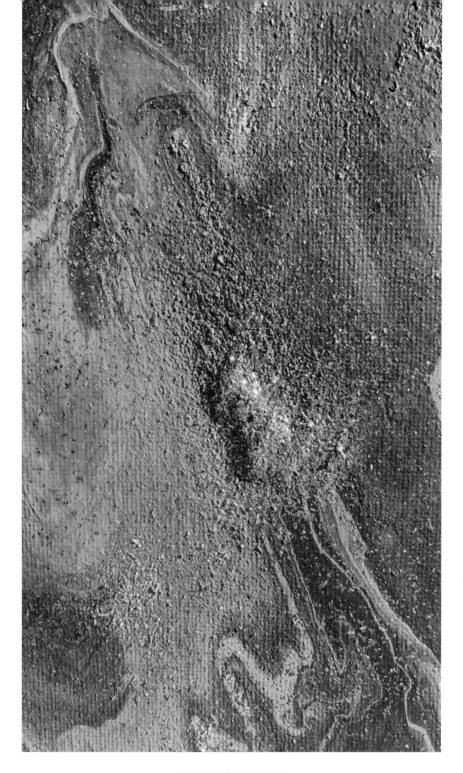

MAYBE SOMEDAY

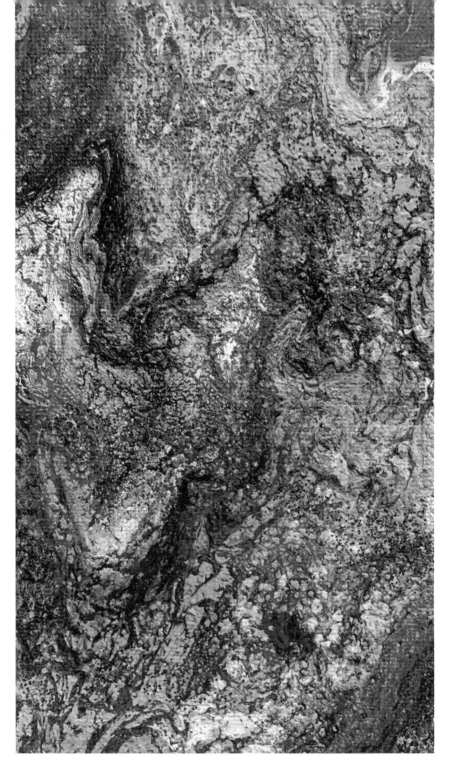

THE PERSON ON THE OTHER SIDE

The Person on the Other Side

Who is the person on the other side of the camera?

Click, swoosh, flash
The wedding, the birthday, the new life

Click, swoosh, flash
Capturing each moment in time

Click, swoosh, flash
A huge event, a brilliant success

Click, swoosh, flash
Watching the lives of others day after day

Click, swoosh, flash
Preserving those precious moments in time

Click, swoosh, flash
It is hard to move from behind the camera
And preserve my own life as I do for everyone else

Click, swoosh, flash

Standing Alone

I
I am
I am alone
I am alone tonight
I am alone tonight watching
I am alone tonight watching the
I am alone tonight watching the stars
I am alone tonight watching the stars way
I am alone tonight watching the stars way up
I am alone tonight watching the stars way up high
I am alone tonight watching the stars way up high wishing
I am alone tonight watching the stars way up high wishing I
I am alone tonight watching the stars way up high wishing I was
I am alone tonight watching the stars way up high wishing I was not
I am alone tonight watching the stars way up high wishing I was not so
I am alone tonight watching the stars way up high wishing I was not so alone.
I am alone tonight watching the stars way up high wishing I was not so
I am alone tonight watching the stars way up high wishing I was not
I am alone tonight watching the stars way up high wishing I was
I am alone tonight watching the stars way up high wishing I
I am alone tonight watching the stars way up high wishing
I am alone tonight watching the stars way up high
I am alone tonight watching the stars way up
I am alone tonight watching the stars way
I am alone tonight watching the stars
I am alone tonight watching the
I am alone tonight watching
I am alone tonight
I am alone
I am
I

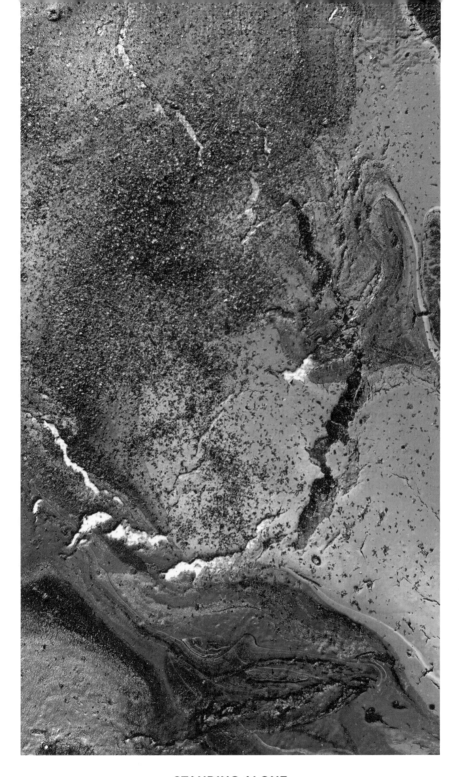

STANDING ALONE

GHOST STORIES

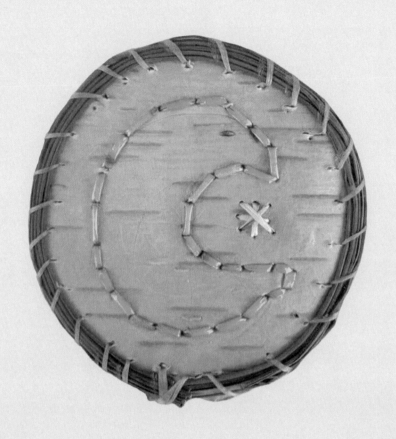

PART TWO

THE GHOST SHIP OF LENNOX ISLAND

The Ghost Ship of Lennox Island

I will warn you—please read this when the sun is high
Now I know you are probably going to ask me why
This is a ghost story from Lennox Island, PEI
Some of you might tremble, some of you might cry
This story might just scare you a bit
So, grab a chair and start reading while you sit
This part will be a tale of a big ghost ship that sails in now and again
None on board should ever be considered a friend
The legend says it came in long ago at the end of its last trip
Don't think they knew where they were going—maybe they had a coin to flip
Old sails it had hoisted up high in the air
Pirates manned this ship through bad times and fair
It sailed to Lennox Island for the captain to bury some gold
Only one man and the captain left to bury it, I was told
The two men started walking around this little Island to find the right spot
I can just imagine the trees and the long grass, it must have been so hot
When the Captain found the place to bury the loot
He commanded the other man, "start digging or I'll shoot"
He pointed the gun straight at his head
"You'll finish this hole or soon you'll be dead"
The man dug and he dug till the hole was all ready
"I'll hand you my treasure now, be careful, and be steady"
When the treasure was set in place the other man came out
The Captain, a greedy man, cut off his head before he could scream or shout
He buried the body, the head, and the treasure all in a flash

When he was done, he thought about his stash
He created a map with little lines and an X
(Yes, I also wondered if this part was a jest.)
So only the captain returned to the ship
His secret would not pass any living man's lips
The body of that poor soul still there with the gold
The ship set sail that night never to return
Did it sink, did the Captain die or did it just burn?
Whatever did happen we will never know
But that Captain comes back on his ghost ship when the tide is low
On quiet summer nights when the tide is out
With the sails all white and fluttering about
You can see a little bit of that ship in the bay
If you listen close you might hear what they say
They don't last long, the visions people see in a fright
It is the captain looking for his loot and his men in the night
An elder told me: once when he was a boy playing in the hole
He found four shiny coins there; he was told they were very old
He thinks it may be a part of that long-lost treasure
Maybe it was, but the truth could sadly be lost forever
Many people have looked for that loot
I have even thought of tracking those boots
That hid the treasure so long ago
If I found it, I would be rich, I know
So, if you want a scare or if you want a fright
Come sit on Lennox Island's shore tonight
And wait for that ghost ship to sail into the bay
If anyone gets off that boat, please just run away!

THE HEADLESS GHOST OF LENNOX ISLAND

The Headless Ghost of Lennox Island

This is my scary tale about the headless ghost
This story I think is the one that scares me the most
It is about an old lady in a dirty white dress who died
I've wanted to find out her story, I've really really tried
What I know for sure is that upon her neck she has no head
I am not even sure if she knows that she is dead
People want to know who she was when she was alive
There are no records around of this lady who died

You can see her on the side of road at night
You have to look for her and try not to take flight
Sitting in a rocking chair moving this way and that
Holding her head on her knee just like a cat
I dare you one day to come see her there
Anyone who sees her has got quite the scare
When I drive by the place where she waits at night
I slow down and look for the lady in white
What does she wait for swaying in her chair?
Is she watching for a young maiden fair?
To maybe help mend her severed head
Or just to figure out why she is dead?

There must be a reason she's still around
And not in heaven or deep in the ground
Does that head have a smile on that old, wrinkled face?
No one looks that long or stays around in that place
I know if you are like me, you'll slow down there to spy
The headless ghost of Lennox Island, PEI

The Haunted House of Lennox Island

I will warn you please read this when the sun is high
Now I know you are likely going to ask me why
Some of you might tremble, some of you might cry
A long time ago a man came to our Island without a spouse
He was the Catholic priest for our St Anne's Church, of course
Throughout the community he became a great force
Sunday mornings he would go around and knock-on people's doors
To church, to church, to church they must go and kneel on the floor
Some loved him, some not so much, but they all came on Sunday
The children loved him, and feared him as well, so they dared not play
In the church, during the sermon when many could not stay awake
For years and years, he lived across from the church in his little house
Some even called him their own little church mouse

When that old priest passed away, strange things soon began
the first people to move in were so scared, they ran
Their first night when they sat down to eat, they could hear walking
Squeak, squeak, squeak
As they put the leftovers away, they could hear someone rocking
Creak, creak, creak
When they went to bed at night, they could hear the knocking
Bang, bang, bang
As they tried to fall asleep, they could hear an old man talking
Mumble, grumble, mumble
They were afraid but they did try to stay
Even though that ghost only wanted them to go away
Soon doors were opening and closing with a bang
Too many pots and pans bashing with loud clangs
The people soon moved out of that haunted house for good
A few people tried to move in after, but moved out as fast as I would

Adults, Elders, and teens, he would torment with his play
Banging and mumbling till they all would run away
But children were different and all who tell this tale will say
He'd never scare a little one, or cause them any dismay
The house sits empty now, only used during the light of day
It is an office, and has been for a while, but even the workers will say
He still comes to visit and play tricks on those who happen to be there
And no one goes down to the basement unless they want a really good scare!
Will he get tired of his tricks and cross over to heaven some day?
Will he stop scaring the people and treating them this way?
For his ghostly behavior can make the strongest warrior weak
For decades now he has given us a great ghost story streak
This is the place that can make you shiver and shake
You can try to sleep there but the ghost will keep you awake

Do you want a real good scare where you just might run and cry?
Come spend some night at the haunted house on Lennox Island, PEI

THE HAUNTED HOUSE OF LENNOX ISLAND

LOST MI'KMAQ GRAVES ON PEI

Lost Mi'kmaq Graves on PEI

When I drove up East here on PEI
A farmer told me a story, just passing by
About some hidden Mi'kmaq graves upon his land
He sat down and told me how this story began
The farmer was very young when his father told him how
When he was a little boy, this story put sweat upon his brow

In a little glen of moss and trees
This Mi'kmaq family fell to their knees
So, they could bury the ones they loved
And say their prayers to the creator above
Sandstone is how they marked the place
Now this family is gone with barely a trace
Who were they and what were their names?
Back then we were thought to be all the same
As I stepped into the glen the world became darker
It was not long before I saw the first red sandstone marker

The wind started to whisper sad Mi'kmaq chants in the breeze
The trees began a dance by rustling their yellow leaves
Had I found some of my relatives here at last?
The farmer's family had protected them generation after generation
From plowing and cutting, but not the endless isolation
I know it is time to bring the people here now
Who have those special machines and know how
To look under the earth to see
Who these people were and help us set them free

What is the story of these lost lonely graves?
Were you a family caught by a terrible plague?
Or were you a family, maybe friends, or a whole clan?
Were you hiding in the woods when everyone else ran?
The stories will come back to us, I hope, someday
Of these people buried in a little glen so far away
I pray your souls are at peace tonight
I hope finding you now makes things right

PRAYERS

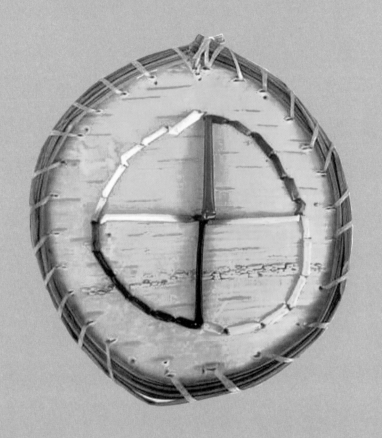

PART
THREE

PRAYER OF THE DAY

Prayer of the Day

When I wake up in the morning I give thanks for the day
For the wonderful things I will hear, learn and say
Today is a blessing, this much I know
I thank you Creator for each day that I grow.
As a child of the deep red earth
I thank the Creator for my birth
When I wake each new day
I smile to myself and I pray
I pray for warm sun in the sky
I pray for the green grass growing so high
I pray for the trees that give me shade
I pray for the bees and the sweet honey they made
I pray for the elders whose wisdom helps our communities
They continue to do this out of love and not just duty
I pray for the youth with hard decisions to make
Please be there to help them choose which road they must take
I pray for the children who don't have a voice yet
Those little ones who need far more than they get
Please give them loving caring arms
And keep them happy and away from harm
I pray for the sick to get well real soon
I pray for the babies still in the womb

I pray for the island so proud in the ocean
I pray for the water the moon sets in motion
With love for my community and family I say
Please hear these simple words right now that I pray
May everyone find some healing and love today
In whatever they hear, whatever they do, whatever they say.

When Things are Bad

When things are going wrong, and you do not know what to do
Ground yourself
When your heart is broken, and your spirit is blue
Ground yourself
When you feel all alone and wish someone was there
Ground yourself
When your self worth is low and your anxiety just seems to grow and grow
Ground yourself
I know the battle that you fight
Each day a struggle to make things right
Ground yourself
Open your heart to try and heal
Ground yourself and breathe
Sit by running water—feel the earth between your toes
Let the negative energy go back into the ground
Your struggle is real with all you endure each day
Know there are hearts that love you,
Eyes that long to see you,
Arms that long to hug you.
You are so loved
And remember when things go bad
Just ground yourself

WHEN THINGS ARE BAD

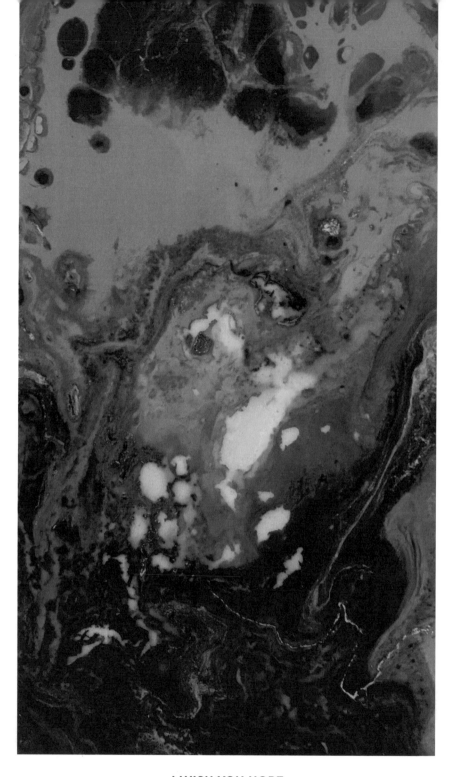

I WISH YOU HOPE

I Wish you Hope

Hope is a mother's heart as she gently
kisses the forehead of her newborn baby.
She is building a wall of love and protection to help keep her little one safe.
That kiss builds a connection of warmth, safety, joy, and love
That will last even after the mother is gone.

I wish you hope

Hope is sitting at the beach watching the setting sun
You hear the sizzle as the sun hits the water
People can believe you or not
You know the stories told from those who walked these shores long, long ago
Stay a little longer, listen a little harder
until you hear the sizzling sound, because you will.

I wish you hope

Hope is looking through glass, waving and smiling at the ones you love
Knowing you cannot hug, kiss, or hold their hands right now.
What we do now will protect them and keep them safe
This isolation will not be forever.

I wish you hope

Hope is the higher being that you talk to when it is quiet, and you are alone.
Or it could be your ancestors who look after you as you continue your path.
No matter who you talk to, keep talking, they are listening,
and they are guiding you.

I wish you hope
Hope is being alone but knowing that you will find comfort soon.
Hope is being scared but knowing help will find you.
Hope is being sad but knowing these feelings will eventually pass.
Hope is being depressed by the dark
and cold of winter but knowing spring will come.

I wish you hope

Hope is knowing in your heart that every day is a new day.
Decisions made, friends and family lost or gained, angry and happy words said
When we go to bed and lay down, we know tomorrow is another day.
It can be full of wonderful adventures and surprising new beginnings.

I wish you hope

Hope is a grandmother's bursting heart when she sees
Her daughter gently kisses the forehead of her newborn baby.
That Grandmother knows she is building a wall
of love and protection to keep her little one safe.
That kiss builds a connection of warmth, safety, joy, and love
That will last even after the Grandmother is gone.

I wish you all hope

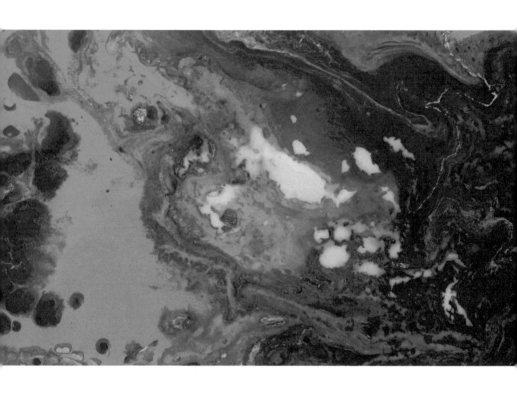

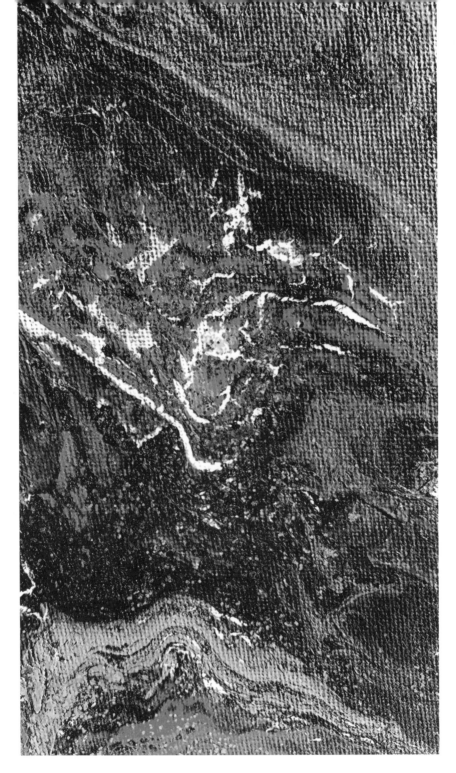

PRAYER FOR THE EARTH CHANGERS

Prayer for the Earth Changers

Creator I humbly pray:
Give my eyes the teaching of truth, so that I can see
what is really there in front of me every day
Give my legs the teaching of humility,
so I know when to stand up and when to sit down
Give my mind the teaching of wisdom,
so I know with clarity what is right and what is wrong
Give my ears the teaching of honesty,
so I can hear the truth, even when it is hard

Give my soul the teaching of courage, so I can be brave to be who I really am
Give my heart the teaching of love,
so I have a reason to stand up for what is right
Give my toes the teaching of respect,
let me learn that all things must be valued
Without toes it is very hard to walk,
so even the smallest of things must have our respect

Give our hands the gift of creation, so we can create beautiful things
Give our mouth the gift of strength,
so we can always say what needs to be said
Give our shoulders the gift of balance,
so we do not get burdened down by things we do not need to carry
Give our fingers the gift of connection—
intertwined to make us strong and ground us to each other.
Let these teachings and gifts come into our bodies,
so we can be true to ourselves and
be the change that the world needs right now.

MY FAMILY

PART

FOUR

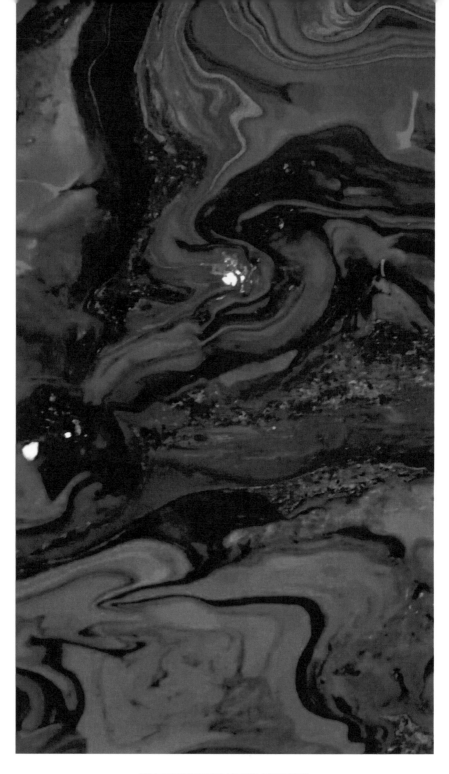

MY MOTHERS BEST FRIEND

My Mother's Best Friend

There is a woman I know of beauty and grace

Her eyes full of stories of times gone by

Her arms hold me tight when she says goodbye

Her lips whisper truths everyone else is scared to say

What would my mother be like if she was alive today?

Would she be happy, sad, or full of pride?

Truly I think she would be like her best friend

Who loves me and stands by me right 'til the end

The Pinecone

The kids brought me a pretty little pinecone today
It smelled like Christmas I just had to say
What is it Mom, they asked me
I could tell they all really wanted to see
This little pinecone is just like you
Tiny and small right now it's true
But if you bury this seed deep in the ground
Very soon a wonderful treasure can be found
In a few years you will see
The beginning of a beautiful huge pine tree
For you, little boys, it is not just soil and sun
With loads of hugs, joy and fun
That will help you grow tall and strong like that tree
To be that vision of beauty that the world will see
That tree will grow branches and thick bark
But you, your arms and legs will start to grow long
And as you grow tall you will also get strong
On that tree little pine needles will start to form
For you, you will get hair to help keep you warm
You are like the pinecone right now children of mine
I know you will grow up and be just fine
You will slowly reach toward the sky
If you were given wings my boys, I know that you would fly
For the tree it should be planted in a quiet little glen
For you, a big house with lots and lots of friends
With sun and rain and the bright red earth
For you little boys, love, and hugs right from your birth
My little ones, you are like the pinecone you found
I know this when I glance around
You will grow up so strong, so fast
Being little just doesn't last
I know you were planted in just the right place
Like that pinecone we now call Grace
To grow and grow up from a seed
My little ones, love and hugs are all you need

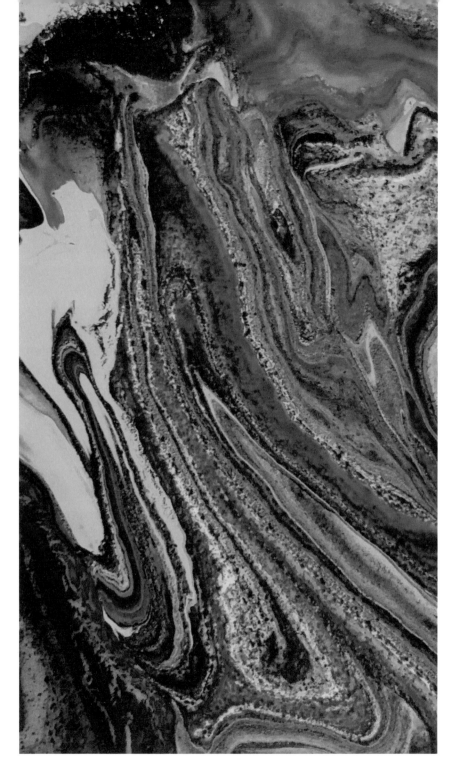

THE PINECONE

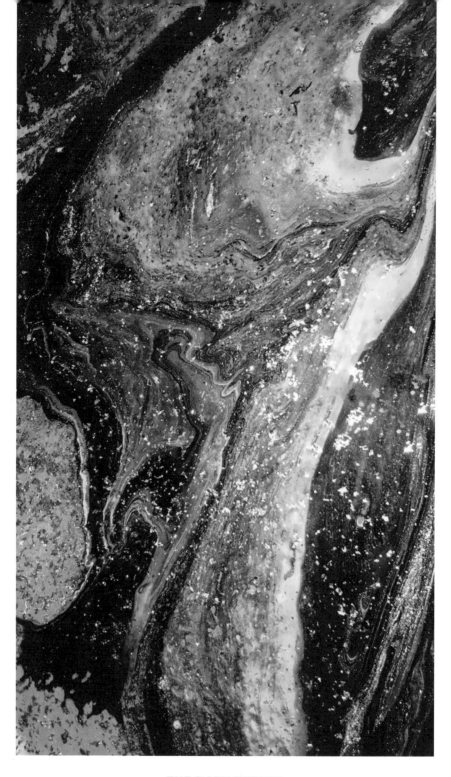

THE BABY WITHIN

The Baby Within

For the little life inside of me today
So many emotions I cannot say
My joy knowing you are safe and warm
Nervous because soon you will be born
I know I've never seemed so complete
Since the first time I felt your body move
Wiggle and kick inside of me, I know you must approve
Your little ways of letting me know you are there
While pregnant I learned people do more than stare
They rub your belly and pretend it is catching
You're a little bird getting ready for hatching

I picture your tiny hands and feet sometimes it's true
I would never hurt you—that would break my heart in two
I love you little one, can't wait to hold you tight
I even want you waking me up through the night
The little sounds you'll make will be music to my ears
I love you little baby, with my whole heart, my dear
I will do everything in my power to be the best Mom I can be
But this is all so new, I know it won't be easy for me

To grow so fast, nine months is not that long
I just need to love, to plan and be strong
And make sure that you will always be my number one
A beautiful daughter or a handsome son
I hope what I do for you here today, deep within me
Will help you grow up strong and proud for the world to see
Will you be a dancer, singer, or drummer when you grow up?
No matter what, you will always be my little buttercup
I ponder these thoughts as I lay in bed at night
Baby, my hope for you is that your future will be bright

One last thing I need to say as I give my tummy a rub
I give you this poem, dear baby, with all my love

My Community

My community of Lennox Island is where I am from
Where everyone knows who you are and who you were
Where people love you unconditionally despite your flaws
They will get mad at you in a heartbeat but get over it just as fast

Where there are few personal possessions, you call your own
Because we know who needs things and we always share
Where one income helps more than one family, because we care
Where one's personal tears become a community's sadness
Where one's personal joys makes everyone celebrate

Where all meals are made with extra, in case company stops in
Be it a birth, death, graduation, marriage, it is time to gather in unity
Where everyone gets a place, and those places hold our community
We do struggle and we do fight
but we will always stand up for each other, that's right

My community of Lennox Island is where I am from
When I go there, I always feel the love
We are more than community
We are family

MY COMMUNITY

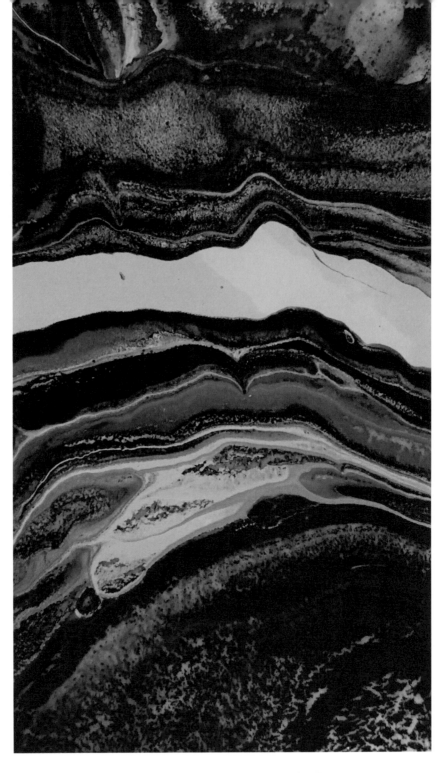

THE HOUSE THAT WAS A HOME

The House that was a Home

There once was a house, right by the beach, hidden in some trees
There lived my Mi'kmaq mother, my father and me
The walls outside were painted a dark forest green
It was the biggest house that I'd ever seen

Two stories high with an attic at the top
I loved my beautiful green house, I loved it a lot
During the summer the flowers grew up everywhere
We were always busy playing in the sun, smelling the fresh sea air

Just outside the house an apple tree grew really tall
We'd pick all the apples before they could fall
Digging clams on the beach for a big clam bake
Eating up so many that my belly would ache

This house was a home full of so much laughter
Full of hope for a "happily ever after"
People always felt welcome; people came and went
All that time just disappeared all that time was spent

One day that Mi'kmaq Mother got sick deep inside
It was cancer, and from that we couldn't hide
She got sicker and sicker as each week and month that went by
Time in that beautiful house went as fast as time could fly

When she passed away on that cold dark morning in March
The house became for us like a broken arch
Each day flowed into another with pain
What was worse, there was no one to blame.

Soon it was sold, and we moved far away
People who bought it just came there to play
Summers when the sun was high in the sky
When winter came, they'd say goodbye

A few years came and went— that house just sat so still
Things started to go once the family had their fill
Soon they came and tore that old house down
They cleared out debris from all over the ground

Now all that remains are the trees standing tall
As though there was never a happy family at all
The house that was a home is not forgotten my me
I stop by and look at that old apple tree

The laugher and love that came from that place
Is not totally gone without a trace
I am here with the memory in my head
The house that was green and the soil that was red

That was my house that became my home
I will return when I stop wanting to roam
Build a house that will become a home
With love and laughter in every stone

The Little Boy with Bright Hazel Eyes

Little boy with the eye of green and brown
You make me smile, even when I am down

You make me laugh; you make me sing
With all the wonderful joy you bring

You may not have grown from my belly at the start
But you grew so much inside my heart

You have grown so big since you came with us to live
Now you run and talk, and have so many kisses to give

Beautiful boy with the bright hazel eyes
When you go back home with your Mom I will surely cry

To see small joys the world has for one so small
Truly little man, you really do have it all

The ten-minute giggle at the sound of your silly giraffe
The great big hugs each time I'm pulled into the room by your laugh

The wonderful stories of Thomas, Pooh and a red balloon
Bedtime is my favorite as we say goodnight to the moon

I give you my heart, little boy with bright hazel eyes
When I am around you the time always flies

With a smile that can light up my every day
You make me want to stay home with you to play

Be a pirate, a King of our little playroom
You make my ordinary gray world just bloom

Colours are brighter, smells are so sweet
A finer two-year-old I could never meet

I did not think I would be changing diapers again
But for you I will do it, my dear little friend

For the little boy with the bright hazel eyes
I will love you forever, no matter your size

When I am old, infirm, and confined to my chair
I hope you know my love for you will always be there

Colours are brighter, smells are so sweet
A finer two-year-old I could never meet

I did not think I would be changing diapers again
But for you I will do it, my dear little friend

For the little boy with the bright hazel eyes
I will love you forever, no matter your size

When I am old, infirm, and confined to my chair
I hope you know my love for you will always be there

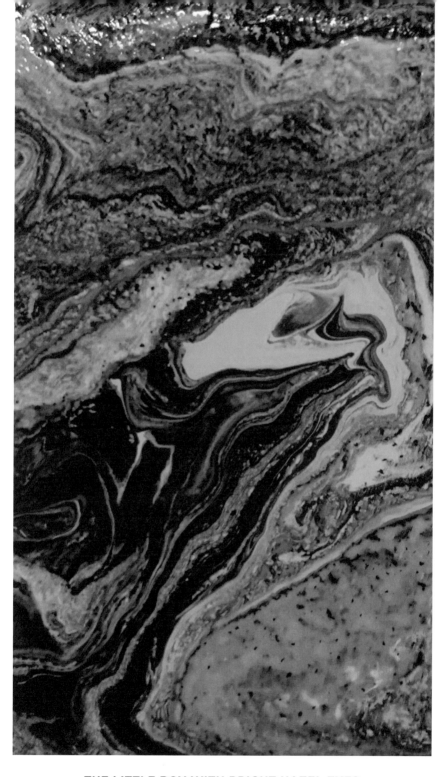

THE LITTLE BOY WITH BRIGHT HAZEL EYES

TAKING A STAND

PART FIVE

WE WILL REMEMBER

We Will Remember

As I sit under the stars with my ancestors
I close my eyes and listen to the sounds all around me
I hear their voices and the stories of the past
We will remember
Maybe it is the Intergenerational knowledge we share
Each cell screaming with the pain that is still there
We will remember
They point to the ones in power that started this whole plan
To end their Indian problem and take away our land.
This part of our history began with one smart but greedy man
We will remember
To try and take away our pride
Make us no longer want to be alive
Take away our children and cause them pain
Treating our women with hurt and disdain
We will remember
Starvation, assimilation, brutality, and all in your name
Breaking our spirits was just a part of your game
We will remember
Our traditions, language, culture, dance, music, and song
Why were they a threat, were they really so wrong?
Did trying to take them away make you feel strong?
We will remember
You will not be remembered for just the great things you did
Our people endured your cruel laws and we lived
We will remember
If I could walk into the past right now, today
I would find him and whisper gently in his ear
Your true story will come out because, we are still here
We will remember

Our Water Song

Water is what I am thankful for
When you have your fill
You will always, always need more
It keeps us clean it keeps us right

Thinking of Mother Earth keeps me up at night

Clean water, clean air is what we all need
To live our lives and put away our greed
With visions of the future not looking so bright

Thinking of Mother Earth keeps me up at night

With our lakes and oceans polluted, the air full of grime
What we've done to Mother Earth is truly a crime
I weep as I think of the next generation
What will be left for them? I shudder with trepidation

Water is what I am thankful for
When you have your fill
You will always, always need more
It keeps us clean it keeps us right

Thinking of Mother Earth keeps me up at night

Mother Earth and Grandmother Moon
We need to listen to you soon
You take care of the water and land
I know this is not what you had planned
Your wisdom and guidance we can trust
The two of you can help save us.

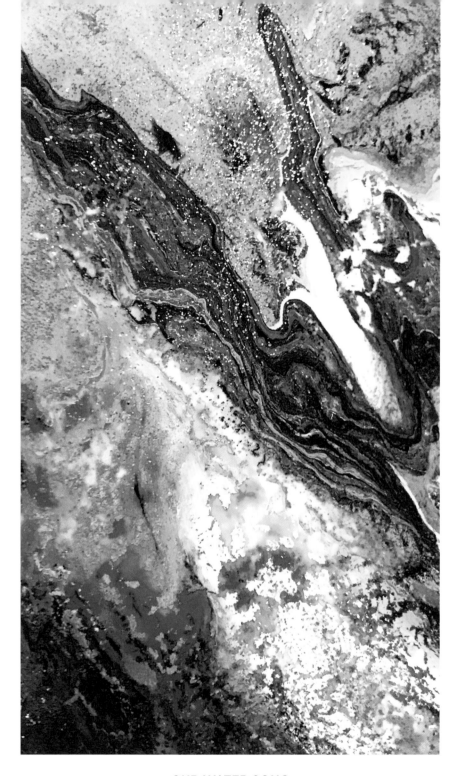

OUR WATER SONG

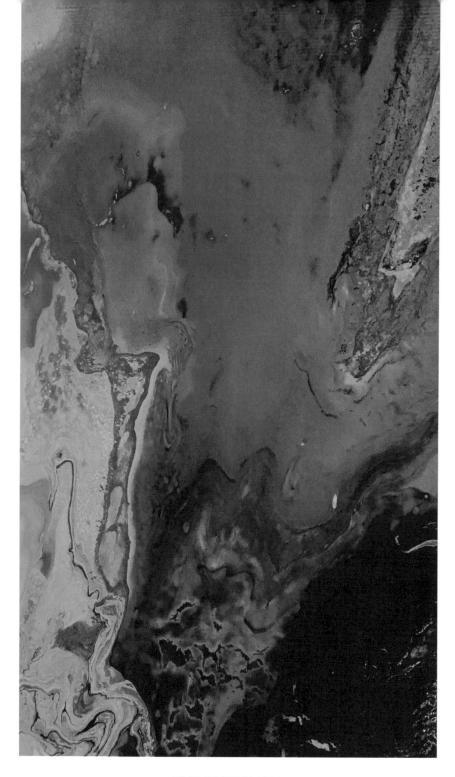

THE DANDELION

The Dandelion

When I say wish, even to myself, that means I still have hope

When I was a little girl, I believed in magic
Wishing upon the first star in the night sky
Picking up every penny I found on the ground
Blowing the fluff from dandelions
Closing my eyes tight as I blew out the candles on my cake
Wishing is my way to keep hope alive

I wish Mother Earth was not in danger
I wish we didn't have to fear any sickness
I wish we could celebrate our differences not fear them
I wish everyone had a past full of joy, not pain
I wish everyone could feel safe in their homes
I wish every child had enough

When I was a little girl, I believed in magic
Wishing upon the first star in the night sky
Picking up every penny I found on the ground
Blowing the fluff from dandelions
Closing my eyes tight as I blew out the candles on my cake
Wishing is my way to keep hope alive

I see the human spirit still alive even during such hard times
I see people who struggle to get the help they need
I see smiles from our elders as we try and keep them safe
I see families finally bonding with the extra gift of time
I see many more babies blessing our Island
I see our artists still reaching out in wonderful ways to bring us joy

Now that I am grown, I still believe in magic
I still wish upon the first star in the night sky
I still pick up every penny I find on the ground
I still blow the fluff from dandelions
I still close my eyes tight as I blow out the candles on my cake
Wishing is and always will be my way to keep hope alive

When we hold our wishes in
We give our hearts room to dream
When we start saying our wishes out loud
We plant the seeds for others to dream

The Four Elements

Air, fire, water, and earth
We need these things since the birth
Of man and animal, bugs, and birds
You must know this, you must have heard
Sacred elements we need everyday
We need these elements to always stay

Air is the element that we can't do without
Without it we cannot breathe, fly or shout
Some of the air is already so bad
Some can't breathe without medicine, it's very sad
How could we do this to the air all around
Soon there won't be a sound
Air's power rules the other elements we know:
It moves the water, shapes the earth and fire; to let us grow
Since I took my first breath, as a baby, I knew
How much we need this element, that much is true

Fire is another of the four sacred elements we say
You keep us warm and energize us, each day
Its flames go through us and give meaning to life
How cold and dark it would it be without fire; such strife
Fire gives us passion and warmth, strong emotions to guide us
That energy creates new life, to look after each other without a fuss
You purify us and everything we need
You help everything grow; even us from a seed

Water comes to us in our lakes, oceans and falling rain
It feeds our hearts, minds and can soothe a soul in pain
To keep our babies safe inside their mother's womb
To bath our elders and keep them fresh so they can bloom
It cleans our bodies, and gives animals and crops a drink
It is so sensitive to what we do, we can lose it in a blink

Earth is underneath us, it is all around
It is our element in the deep red ground
Mother Earth gives us the soil of dark red
When we pray to her, she hears what we've always said
She is the womb of all our plants and trees
That feeds us, the animals, the birds, and the bees
We need to give her love, and protect her from harm

When things can't grow any more, it is cause for alarm

Four elements we have, and we need them all today
We give thanks for each and hope they're here to stay
The creator gave them to us to be the caretaker to all
We lost our way, but now we know this is our call

Four elements that make us strong and keep us all alive
Four elements that give us life, help us to grow and thrive
Think of them as you awake for the day
Think of them as the sunlight fades away

The youth will always be the first to see
The elders will always remind me
To watch for the signs that are dire
So, there will be no day without water, earth, air, and fire

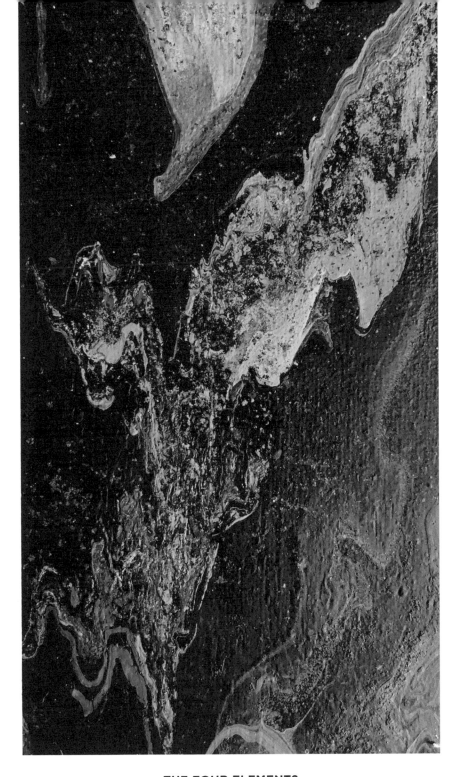

THE FOUR ELEMENTS

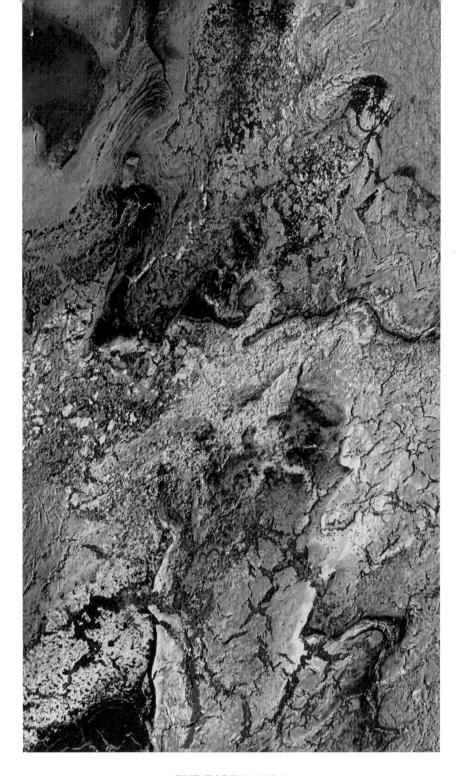

THE EARTH AND I

The Earth and I

When I see the beauty in the earth, I shudder with delight
When I see the cruelty in the earth, I cry with all my might
As I look outside my window, I watch the snowflakes passing by
I wonder if they notice me, as they float from their home up in the sky

Each snowflake is unique as it falls and flutters by
But once it hits those piles of snow, it becomes just the same as I
Blending in like the millions of other people on Mother Earth
With limited time to shine and make change

The summer has its good points when the days were warm and new
To swim in the bright clear water and sail in a birch bark canoe
To sit and dream of love while staring at the moon
But when the heat becomes oppressive, we wish for snow then too

This time for dreaming is over, the winter brings the ice and cold
The bitter cold brings reality yet does not make a sound
Now the dreams we all believe in start with money in the bank
Not of children's laughter, joy, love, or people we should thank.

To look outside our selves and give help to those in need
To be the people we should be or even plant the seed
To love and protect the world and all its creatures would be a start
These things to help the Earth must come straight from your heart.

Be the snowflake that flutters from the sky, full of beauty and hope
Be the one that makes a difference, be the one who becomes the change

Protectors of the Earth

We fight for our earth
We fight for our water
We fight for our air
We fight for our fire
We fight for the next seven generations

The earth is our home, where we all live
She is like our mother who gives us life

The ground is her flesh, it nourishes us and helps us grow
The grass is like her hair, moving to and fro

The water is her blood, keeping her healthy and strong
When we hurt any part of her, we should know it is wrong

We must do better, and surpass our traditional expectations,
We must ensure she stays safe for the next seven generations

We need to stand up, and shout to raise the alarm
For all to protect her, and keep her safe from harm

We fight for our earth
We fight for our water
We fight for our air
We fight for our fire
We fight for the next seven generations

PROTECTORS OF THE EARTH

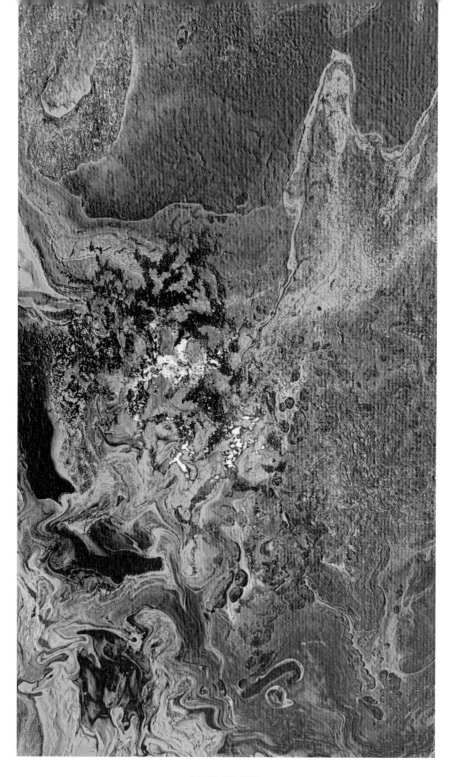

I BELIEVED

I Believed

I believed everyone was treated equal
I believed everyone had access to all they needed
I believed everyone had a childhood full of fairy tales
I believed that when you were old there was always somebody there

I don't believe that anymore

I believe we must fight for equal rights for everyone
I believe that even here in Canada, we do not all have access to what we need
I believe we must protect the children who wake up cold,
hurt, hungry and afraid
I believe we can all have access to clean water, clean air, and good food
I believe we can learn how to help those who cannot help themselves

The Elders who need love and someone to be there
The children who need us to notice those blank stares
I believe someday we can all be equal, it's not that hard

I do believe

Why we take a Stand

As First Nations People all over this land
What makes us act and take a strong stand?
Is it lack of education, poverty or abuse?
Is it programs created that we can never use?

Put in isolation on reserves, away from urban places
House built close to the next house, running out of spaces
This can be where relationships get stressed and sad
People get angry and they start acting bad

Some take drugs or drink booze to take away the pain
Wondering where their pride has gone, when only hurts remain
Useless fighting where blood is spilt
Sometimes people are even killed

Loved ones are always left to grieve
Many stay and only a few ever leave_
Women hurt badly by familiar faces
Forced to hang out in those same dark places

Pretending the pain isn't really there
Bruises hidden under the clothes they wear
Why is there so much pain for this generation?
The elders are hurt with all this information

The government comes in to consult
Over and over and over, it's an insult
Can we find the answers locked inside these uncaring rooms?
What can they do to help heal these wounds?

WHY WE TAKE A STAND

Taking our words down with care and then they turn and go
What happens to these words? Well, I really do not know.
Nothing is ever done, the troubles never end
But we can smile and always try to pretend

Who can save us from these complicated things?
Give us solutions and help us find our wings
The government's system's laws and rules?
The elders' culture and storytelling tools?

The little children in the system who need things to change?
All the people who are damaged and act very strange?
Is it up to every community member?
Spending an hour or two just being together?

I wish I had the answers now
I wish I had an idea how
To help all the people in isolation
Regenerate with love and not degradation

What these problems won't take away
Is our love for each other, the respect that we pay
We share what we have, no matter how many
We will always give to those who don't have any

These problems are not new, they are just mountains we must climb
We need some answers now, so we can fix it again this time
Communities are who we are, all across this land
Isolated and lost sometimes, but that is why we take a stand

The Shell and the Sand

Hurt seeps into your soul like the water in the sand
Just as you think it is gone away, another wave comes in
It fills every space and leaves no oxygen
There is no air, just swirling water as the waves keep crashing in
Poor dear sand

Sometimes hurt is like a small shell on the shore
Being lifted, thrown this way and that
Sometimes landing high enough to think you are safe
But you are not, get pulled back in, time and time again
Poor dear shell

Little shell, while you are in the waves you can see the sand below
Watching it gasping for air, looking desperately at you for help
But it is not you who can save it, not you who can change things
It is only time and tide that can save you both
Poor dear sand and shell

When my community is in pain, we are the sand and shells
Feeling the hurt of a Nation with no power to heal this pain
Watching our people suffer these uncovered truths
As the stories told by our survivors are now proven
Poor dear lost souls that never made it home

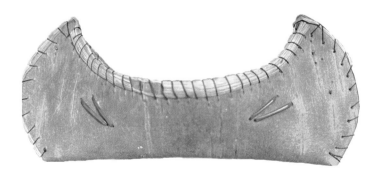

THE SHELL AND THE SAND

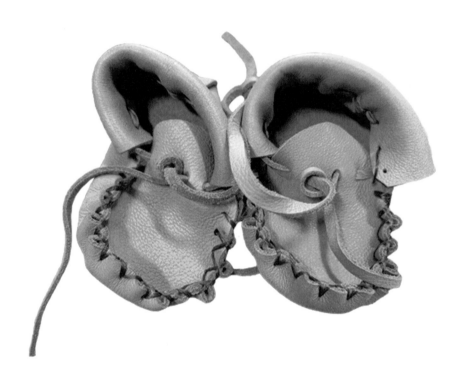

THE APPLE TREES

The Apple Trees

In the wind I hear their voices:
Look for us now so we are not alone
It is time for us all to finally go home

Children taken from our families and homes
We had no choice but to cry goodbye and go
These places were always dark, scary, and bad
Whatever we did, someone always got mad

At night, our sobbing began without end
All of us children just needed a friend
We were not seen as human, so easy to be hurt
When we died we were buried deep in the dirt

They ended the lives of us little one's time and again
There was no sadness when our bodies shut down
They buried us always late, late at night
There was no one to tell them this was not right.

An elder told me what he learned as a boy
Something that slowly took away all his joy—
Apple trees they planted on those sad little graves
Those trees hid their crimes, no need to be afraid

Look for the trees full of apples near the schools
These helped those monsters break all their rules
The tree roots run so deep in the ground
They hide all those bodies, so they wouldn't be found

Indigenous people all over this land
All know the stories. We have taken a stand—
It is now, it is time, come listen to our truths
Bring all our children home from beneath those choking roots

Creator help us, let the winds of change blow
This is our living history, not long ago
Listen for the little voice screaming, "Please remember me."
We must now go and look for those sad old apple trees

For those children who never made it home
My Heart shatters that you were so alone
For those children full of trauma, who are still alive
Please don't ever feel guilty for being able to survive

It is the time to sit with our survivors now
And if they need help do not be afraid to ask them how—
They hold the truths they would much rather hide
Of all those other children who did not survive

In the wind I hear their voices,
"Look for us now so we are not alone
It is time for us all to finally go home"